Wrong Feast

First Edition

ISBN-13: 978-1-936097-72-2
Library of Congress Control Number: 2026942630

Baobab Press
316 California Ave, 24
Reno, Nevada 89509
www.baobabpress.com

WRONG FEAST

poems

Rivka Clifton

BAOBAB PRESS
RENO · OMAHA

Contents

"I try to write you a love song but it comes out a lament"

—St. Vincent

"Blessed are those who stand still in their confusion"

—Brigit Pegeen Kelly

ע

Consumption

A catfish ought to be gut
a few hours after it dies.
In a parking lot on my tailgate,
I made the cut, plied back
the flesh. In the stomach,
a few dollars were neatly
folded and steeped in blood.
It was not the first time
I saw potential in the body.
My mother was half-way
across the country, telling
a nurse about her downstairs
neighbor, how he bugged her
phone and put a microscopic
camera in her bathroom.
Just below the streetlight
inside a black bulb, a camera
watched my knife tap the fish's
skull as the glass doors
of the Chevron-McDonalds
coughed out the new money
who bought several properties
on the lake and planned to
invest until nothing remained
untouched. I knew my mother
was going to die just as I knew
the rhythm of digits flowing
in and out of my bank account.
A few dollars would not do
much. A few weeks without me
would not kill her. Though,
under this sign, I wondered
how to detangle cash and flesh.

The Master in Pieces

A dog ran through the park. He was not a dog but a man in a dog mask. Leather gesture, enough to signal. I, too, wore a mask. We all did and do; the world is sick that way. His handler tossed a ball, and he fetched. He acted like a dog and wore that face.

The human face hooded, zippered into a yawping muzzle, the eyes expressed what they felt. Across the green, the dog with the body of a boy on all fours. Away from his handler and back. His handler tickled his ear.

Good boy. The leather hood bobbed as the dog trotted back to his handler; the metal bits of his harness and collar rung. I pretended not to watch. I jingled the quarters in my pocket—heads over tails, tails over heads.

The dog rolled over to expose his belly. The handler rubbed the dog as a dog handler would before snatching the ball and tossing it, farther than before. The dog took off after the ball, in search of the affection to come.

They adhered to the set of rules agreed on in advance. Is this not a start? To define what is wanted from another, from oneself, one has to pretend to be the desired. It was getting late. Neither wanted to stop. It was too dark, so they agreed, a final toss.

The dog bolted. The face his face. The two as one. Running across the park, how beautiful he was, how beautiful the handler running after. Like men and not, like dogs and not, like chasing the one chasing the other chasing the mutable night.

Who Are Americans

I saw a man in the dark.
So what? I said. A man
can lurk, can do his junk
there in the dark, and why
do I care what another man
does. I said I saw what
I saw — him and the hunting
gear in the morning, he
like his hunting gear, flashed
stark and white. He carried
the gear, its ungodly gleam.
That's right, I said to
an emergency responder,
a camouflaged man moved,
flashing teeth. Did he
not wish to be seen? I saw
and so said something.
In the dark and in
the morning. I said a thing
about ashes and dust. Why
the gleam like teeth. The gear
in the truck. It peeked
above the bed, readied,
loaded. Morning rose
above the truck. I said that
morning I saw a man. Who
was he to be doing his junk
so early and in the dark?
I asked myself. Should I
alert the authorities? I had
not spoken to the man.
No, not for a long time.
He went about his mornings.

I went about mine. I pulled
the weeds — how quickly
they multiply. One thing,
the next. And the world is
overrun. Often he sat on
his porch, talking loudly,
practically shouting into his
cell phone. Did he say, *Deluge,*
the morning? I read about God
growing weary of violence
and so committing violence.
I saw him that morning.
Loading his truck. So what?
I said and meant it. He drank
his coffee. He drove, hunted.
Was he dangerous? This man,
my neighbor? Was he weary?
The righteous walk with God
and float above retribution.
He lifted several bags
into his truck. I saw him.
In the dark, hunting gear —
in the morning a man and
in the morning another man.

The Suspended Body

We were introduced through a friend
at her house party. It was high school,
and I can't remember what happened
to her. We stepped outside and she said,
This is K. She gestured to a slight man,
a boy, who turned to us from the lawn.
His body wounded the dusk, and I felt
compelled to rub the dark spot he cast
until it healed into a scar, the kind
that brightens in a hot bath, a forget-me-
not of blood beneath skin. We shook,
exchanged numbers. I left. In high school,
I could twist in and out of experiences.
I drove to one house where I laughed.
I drove to another and sat silently until
finally we thrust our mouths against each
other like carp at a dock. I did this often,
and often in the short term I forgot
one night or conflated a few. Then, months
later, like the sharpened teeth of road kill
suddenly visible—my body splayed on
the dark wheel of a trampoline, blooming
smoke in the sweet spot of my mouth.
Yes, every part of my body is appalled
by the relish with which it took to this.
At home and late, my phone shook.
It was K. He asked me to join him
in the city. It was raining. It hit
the asphalt and turned into mist.
I shimmied out the bedroom window
and into my car. I drove to the city,
where streetlights hung above those
who lounged there—sequined jackets,

mini-skirts. The light moved its anxious
finger across a neck, over a temple,
coming to rest in eye-shadow. I stared
until they returned my stare; my face
turned in theirs to a morning glory's.
K said he could get us in without ID.
The bar hummed with bass, distorted
and dull like the sound of a thumb.
I inhaled the friction's sweet smell,
the rancid bud of gathered sweat.
K pulled me up the stairs. In the dark
the breakbeats let loose their strobe.
K's face twisted into a mess of pleasure.
I turned to see a shape ahead. It phased
in and out with the lights like a figure
in a dream or the illusions that float
in the dark when the body is ready
for a dream but the mind stays pinned
awake — unwinding the ceiling until
it is a thousand tangling bodies searching
for a mate. Ahead, a bound body,
naked, the rapid strobe pumping
our pupils. He hung suspended
by an unseeable wire. Belly pulled to
the ceiling, shoulders arched, head
dangling. The body turned in red light,
a fine orchid, a ghost washed in blood.
I watched K. His eyes turned on
the wire. Another figure stroked
the body with a feather. He tugged
a glistening chain. I felt K move closer
to me. His slight frame and mine
jostled past each other's. His face

brought close. My mouth slackened.
But he did not cover it with his, did
not tongue my tongue. So I pushed
my wet mouth toward his. He recoiled.
It never occurred to me until then
how similar tongue and flower are.
His face was an overgrown field,
his tongue the sought after fleshy petal.
I wanted to hold it for the wind to wag
(the ecstatic word, the trembling syntax),
but no wind blew, and I did not move.

To Bury Everything

The residency had ended. Most of the artists were gone. Because of an unforeseen delay, I was stuck there. I didn't mind. I wandered the half-emptied and darkened galleries—the lights were on timers. But one stray beam can give the brain enough. Paintings turn to mirrors. Every piled installation becomes a crouching figure, and every figure comes alive—glittering surfaces like the unseeing eyes of the dead. One artist spent the week remaking Louise Bourgeois' *Arch of Hysteria* from stuffed pantyhose. We spent a long time discussing the original and their multiple homages to it. They said pantyhose was the ideal material—feminine but also meant to hide the feminine. The original was polished bronze. Wherever it was displayed, it lit the room with the light it reflected. When I first saw it, I stared at its exaggerated bend, how my reflection distorted around the folds of fingers, feet, the protruding pelvis. Hard and heavy, it did not move on its steel cable. These arches made the opposite gesture: soft, pliable, ghostly. Lifting them was like lifting the elderly, those near death. Once I was charged with moving my mother from her bed to her wheelchair. I remember how little it took to scoot her over the edge. During the residency, I worked in unfired clay. I made elaborate urns. I left them outside for the rain and dew to digest before hauling them back in to display as collapsed vessels, failed receptacles for the failed body. Earth to earth. Unlike the original, the arches did not gleam. Holding one by its thread, the artist believed the arc it made was from the wear they put into the pantyhose. *This is how I would bend*, they said, *if I were suspended.* They took my hand and traced the sculpture's limp parabola. Too much touch and it twirled on its string. They stuffed it taut with cotton and cash. Everywhere bulged: the ends, the joints, the crotch. When restrained just right, money can ghost the body, can turn it to dirt and ash. I looked at the arches so much I felt I knew their every inch. My mother died years ago. Now when I thought of her, she was a cut-out and moved like a cut-out, floating stiffly through memories like some flat ache longing approximates. I remembered our time together when I walked through the galleries—me and this artist. We installed our work in the same small room. I stood in the doorway. The lights from the parking lot filtered through the hall's windows. They cast long, flat rivers of grey. In the dark, the room looked empty. I shifted side to side, up and down, trying to find an angle that would hint at the many arches in the room and the many urns behind them. I wanted to see them one last time. I reached into the dark and felt along the wall. Thinking I found the switch, I pulled down, and the sprinklers released.

A feast of small proportions

can hardly be called a feast. More of a delicacy. But even that fails
to describe the meager plates set out on the long, dark oak.
The misty room glowed. In the corners, the wait staff like stiff, black branches,
and momentarily I was confused. In my hand my keys, a snapped antenna
picked from the curb, a clean fork.
All meal long, the brain tucked in its dome and the heart cubed,
presented on six white plates. The meat, almost raw, slid around,
and I grabbed a piece. I brought it to my mouth. Everything went metallic.
My hipbones tipped their empty bowls.
My hand pressed to my chest then curled into itself like the slowed
glittering legs of a dying cockroach. But the heart, how delicate!
How marbled its rotting honeycomb!
The heart is filling, even when small. Especially then. I finished and felt
the earth in my stomach. If I moved it would pour out
as an entire hive, in the height of spring when the field is set
with little feasts. Blossoms opened, glowing like a body
when the heart has been taken by another—licked until tender—and then
carried away by a waiter whose unbuttoned jacket spreads its shimmering wings.

Who Cannot Place Themselves in the Soul of the Hunter?

The mosquitoes undulate closer.
Yes, the heart is an empty muscle.
Its ventricles fill with blood.
The hand slaps the back a few
times as if to say *congratulations*
to itself. Each mosquito wears
the coat of a previous mosquito.
They fly by one another. They tip
their top hats without a thought—
like they've met before. They have.
But the heart has no fingerprints.
One can never be known
from the other. A hammering
in the chest's dark warehouse.
A mosquito inside the body is
a mosquito at work. Its heart
a mess with everything it must
consume. It quivers, empties.
Then fills. Its red orb floats.

The Dark Radio

The radio devolved into static. I listened intently, my finger on the SCAN button I did not press. Soon, the static parted. The car radio like an unseen brain deep in the reeds. It let me in on a secret. It mimicked my voice. It said, *the world is small and the people are grave.* The imitation was not very good. It got my voice wrong. I listened intently. The radio devolved. Static in unseen circuitry. My finger on SCAN was the partition between my volition and my vehicle. The engine an organ, not a very good one. My brain devolved into static. I listened intently. The blips mimicked my voice. Was it so bad? It let me into the radio's overgrown mess. It said, *the world is small and grave.* I processed. I devolved. The vehicle listened intently to its own churning. The blips came closer. The SCAN button's jump-cuts. My brain processed the radio into its own channel and said, *the world is a small grave for small people.* My finger on SCAN, my brain a mess of reeds sprouting from an abandoned car's soiled upholstery. The vehicle devolved. The car radio was getting better. I let it in on the secret to my voice. I gave it a channel in my brain. Static and my voice. I processed the jump-cuts. The radio listened. I said, *small grave, small world.* My brain listened to static. I agreed. A secret pumped through the vehicle. SCAN beneath my finger asked, *is the world the world of a small grave?* Is it the jump-cuts of an unseen question? I did not press it.

Receive with Simplicity Everything that Happens

Knocking at the door, my mother
just beyond
the awning explained nightmares follow

late meals. She admired the snow. *What a marvel*
she said, *snow in Florida*. It fell a long way
through the dark to cling to her.

*

In a gust of wind, there is no wind.
Rashi wrote something like that

in a very large tome.

*

Through the radio, a singer croons he can't help it
if he cries. He tells me to sleep,

that in dreams we can walk and talk
with anyone we wish.
The waves of his voice caress the black cloth

of the ionosphere before falling back,
filled with snow, to earth.

*

Across the path the snow slid through itself like shed skin,

a thumb across the crisp edge of a wad of cash.

                                        I wanted to feel
if it were real, so I got close — ice flapped over
ice. The rabbi said, *The wealth of tradition*

will get you through grief in the hospital.
It was snowing. It felt so valuable, so weightless.

*

A black curtain draped over a wooden fence

pulsed like a dream during our waking
                                                        hours. *Sleep*
said the clock as its hands drifted further apart.

*

                                        In the dark, my mother
peeked over the ledge of my bedroom window.
Only in dreams, in beautiful dreams

                                        the radio wheezed
as its battery waned and it fell asleep. She had been
falling ill for what seemed like forever.

*

Sleep like the black cloth
of a trampoline hauled out and held under

a ledge. In the air, my mother's constant fall,
her hands at midnight and noon.

Her fingers extended
as if pointing at an important passage
scrolling into the sky.

The Dad

In a grocery store, the dad holds his son's head together.
A hand under the chin and the other covering the crown,

he applies pressure; he feels his son's teeth shatter
the coffee bean he dropped into his mouth like a pill. His son swallows.

His son vibrates down the aisle. The dad follows. He waffles before a wall of cereal.

His son talks to another man, also called dad. The dads
exchange looks. They both reach out to clasp
the other's outstretched hand. Another dad turns the corner. He nods.

At home, one dad thumps a tire with his heavy lug wrench. One dad tells his son to get back

in the house or else. One dad brings a pile of smoldering leaves to his face
and inhales. The dads ask each other unremarkable questions. *Does being*

a dad change you? Being a dad changes you. Sure, somewhere
a mother. Sure, a large sheet fits across their large mattress.
The dads undulate with breath. They share a single body. They come together,

then they split. They come together. Their bed rocks. They respond
to a text from the mother. *Sure*, they type. The message sends. The message stays in place.

Cyclist with a Parachute

Thighs and calves bulge under Lycra. The parachute: a nylon bag gorged on air. A thick strap attaches it to the cyclist, and pedal clips attach him to the bike. In silhouette, no difference between conduit and force. The man strains; the parachute expands. Does he move forward? Do the wheels turn? For a moment I do not think so. But they must to keep the cyclist upright. It is good to think he would stay upright—his pedaling, the wind—, to think *balance* a synonym for *eternity*. But the cyclist does not stay upright. He falls. His parachute deflates. I assumed in falling the bicycle, man, and parachute would stay attached as if made from one stiff piece of matter, that the cyclist with a parachute would rest on the ground a moment before rising all at once like a metal figure in a shooting gallery—dead then alive, having never lived. The world is so far from what the mind devises. The cyclist twists out of the pedal clips. The parachute droops. The tail that steadied deflates. The man lies there, separated from his bicycle. Who is he now? More man, less chimera. What is he now? Stiff, rising. A pain shoots through his ankles and knees, which now hold bits of gravel. He hobbles. Under his quarter-zip, his chest heaves. His parachute drags.

ע

In Florida

—for my mother

My mother died a few days earlier.
It was not the summer I asked for.
In the yard, I stared: gnats in black
clouds, barely visible in the evening;
my neighbors coming home, racing
to click their doors shut. The peach
tree stood, half-dead, without a single
fruit. I was still, but the tree was not.
The bark wriggled in a cold sweat.
I asked for a summer with days
that oozed from the night's unyielding
hive. I asked for so long, *Will she live,*
will she get up and walk? Time started
my concerns—neither the action nor
the consequence in mind. I looked
more intently. Then there was no *then*.
The bark dripped and rose—a stirring
beneath. What wiggled up and down
the tree's spine like two thoughts
telling the brain *no more* and *is it time?*
I left my mother at hospice to wash
her nightgown, to return it clean
so she could sleep. *And then*, I say.
So much depending on the layering
of action, what was and what will be.
But not on the tree that wiggles—
the leaves' shuddering, the bark's
drip-rising, my mother's hobbling
from car to wheelchair to a bed
that adjusts with a button. How
could the tree move without moving?

I inched closer; ants marched into
its leaves, into the grass, the dark
tunnels. No moment between steps
for ants, no here or there. Each
moment interchangeable with the next.
Also not what I asked for — my living
mother and my dead both wriggling.
Not the soiled nightgown, not that
alone, not the clean one in my hands.
I wanted a past cemented — the mind
fixed in the present. Nothing could
call it back to when time began
my every sentence — *when, when, when* —
only to melt into the dead, to become
less than those who experience no time,
like ants who go from A to B and back
as if in one moment. So full of time,
I forgot how all beings can bloom
and wither without considering who
and why — my mother and the ants
going back inside the earth outside.

Metastatic

I walked on shadows. Shadows like any other: heartless spaces, invisible buttons, deadly traps. Inside I felt the shadow's heart. In the shadow's heart, a hank of hair, a sleeping spool. I grabbed the hair. It dangled from my fingers. The light licked the hair. The hair squirmed. I dropped it and ran. The hair coiled. It was mine, and I lost it. I rushed back. No hair. No trace. No irradiated blood to light my way. Hardly recognizable, the shadow stared up about to speak.

The Complicated Thing

We found it in the junk drawer. I held it to the light, admiring the precision. You tapped your phone and jotted down numbers while it lay outstretched on the opposite side of the table. I touched its scabbed muzzle. It grunted. In the other room, you buried your face in its soft torso. The sun cut a line across its belly. We stuffed it in a latex suit and controlled its breathing with an intricate series of tubes. We wedged its head between wheel and concrete then slowly rocked back and forth in the front seat. I took my heel to it. I let it starve over a weekend. *What do we do*, I asked, *with the body?* You slapped it on the cutting board and chopped off the fat. The oil sizzled so loudly I couldn't hear what you said. In the morning, it shuffled across the tile, toenails clicking out of sync with its wheezing. We locked it in a freezer and left it for the city to haul away. We were very sad. Our faces soaked in the TV light. I wondered what weapons it had pulled from its pockets—we all knew the statistics, we all knew someone. You palmed my face and pointed outside. The locks had broken. It tore down the alley as if a storm were in tow, barking its lungs out, showing its brains to anyone who looked. You saw a shadow followed by another shadow trot through the neighborhood. We raised our hands when it approached. Without emotion, we said we had no cash. I barely recognized it—standing far off, teetering on the curb, encased in a sweatshirt. It said, *That's not what I meant at all.* You nodded; I nodded. You ran up to greet it. You asked it inside, gave it the garden shed to sleep in. It raised its head like a dark plume over the city.

Imagining a Thing that Does Not Look like a Ghost

The filmstrip folded through the projector; shot across the room—
the image: a nail impaling a foot over a pitcher of milk.

Tilted as if into a mouth. One nested inside the other: the city and the suburb,
the house and the room, the brain

and the long trenches a claw hammer dug into the plaster.

The house's dark muscles shifted. A storm massaged the house into place—
its music when bowed just right. The crescendo of touch. Of pleasure turned into pleasure

with pain and then to pain. I popped a knuckle, a vertebra and exhaled.
The house's upturned face swelled, the overture of demolition. All the strings hummed

their own unraveling. A thousand voices sang. The phrases rung as if through a chain.

It, too, was a pleasure to score the house with a soundtrack meant for another place.
I thought how similar the sounds *score* and *scour* and the action, too.

The conductor's wrist, the hand rubbing a spot,
the knife through dough, eye tracing and retracing—they all dig in,

weigh on the brain like an oversized locket dangling from a chain. A deadweight—
as in the dead waited inside

Across the wall, the image of a mirror reflected the camera without an operator. Dead
center, the white dot of the mirror within

the camera stared at the eye scouring the eye within the mirror. In my brain,

a dying pulses its distress signal. I turned the projector and like a chemical dust blown
across the landscape it lit the backyard. Its milky sliver

flowed down the window's single tooth. Within my brain, the two superimposed.
What was there? Projector and filmstrip. The eye inside the ruptured eye.

Scarlet Heaven

An Itoh peony begins as an eye—it awakens. The yellow petals peel from the vibrating pupil. On screen, it blinks. A bulb of worry, a brain consuming itself. How much does a pixel cost the environment? Who will see it moving and the burning behind its movement? The flower's red mouth opens, and its worries shift around. Loose yellow teeth. The flower tongues its yawning petals. It is so full of itself. Compressed like an organ in a ribcage. The sutures loosen. Fire pours out its golden hair. The Itoh peony is a drop of blood with an ember inside. It's a corpse on a conveyor belt to a cremator—the flames glow within the square hole across the concrete room. The flower spreads its bloodless wound. It shows the yellow pearls of fat that glitter in the crematory's eerie light. Maggots that sizzle into oil. A larger destruction whirs overhead. Lifting away, the peony reveals inside itself a single room—an extended family sitting around a table. The moving geometry of getting up, taking a spot, coming back, quibbling over possession. Aunts and uncles writhe in laughter. A child falls, is swarmed by other children. A parent points outside. Someone leans in and remarks on death or the difficulty one faces in the evening behind the screen trying to capture a bird in motion above the tall grass. The Itoh peony pinches like a cul-de-sac. People file into the street. Music, quiver. They talk about a recent storm, the power outage that drained the city of resources. One by one streetlights flickered. Then men in bright yellow vests came. They milled about their trucks. They chainsawed the debris and carried it away. The city reopened. How long can any catastrophe keep us occupied? Today, highway traffic flutters a petal outside while inside a peony, a pulsing border. The earth dilates—white-filmed, bloodshot it looks at a screen where an Itoh peony dulls out its red drone.

The Dybbuk

The ear and the mouth move
in sync. The voice won't come

if the tongue is wrong.
First of all, the soft becomes

solid, possessing,
possessed, wrapped

in the throat's moist shawl.
The more reckless the talk

the further the speaker from their body—

as if a knife severed the two
and feathered the flesh. Oil

would encase it.
And fire. Fire if it felt

like it. It would do it. It would
show there were always two—

one mouth pressed to another's
ear. It's like nothing

is inside. But there is.

To Swallow the River That Spews from the Mouth

Someone hid the fountain in a corner
of their backyard, covered it with junk,
but I could see it, through the chain-link

fence. New to the neighborhood, I walked
by often. Often in dreams I saw the shape:
three concrete fish entwined, slurred.

A single fish. Bodies like tubes of muscle
sheaved in scales, their wriggle slowing
at the base of heads bent perpendicular

to the bodies, mouths full of wolves' teeth.
The gills' repeating frame, coral and bone.
The gullets pulsed as the fish inhaled me.

Then winter, spring, and the yard was bare
except the fountain. It stood in the corner.
It sulked. Maybe it was too heavy to move.

Or connected to a water main and needed
a professional to sever and seal its innards.
Doubtful, but the world can still surprise.

A thick spout protruded from each throat.
Along the spouts, pooling in grooves
on the tongues, and spilling over the lips,

green algae dried black like a walnut husk
decaying into the ground. All who touch
this pigment wither, but the seed, its flesh

sustains. In time, flesh rots. Even stone.
The fish, pockmarked by weather. No telling
the skill of the fabricator's hand, if there was

a hand, if there were only this one defunct
fountain or many around the world spitting,
distorting the glance of those who look

into the pool above which the fish appear
to leap like how a hand is bent by still water but
appears to bend itself into something else

and is unrecognizable, made even more so
by the ripples of the spouts' trickling.
The additions, water and water, blur what is

into its parts. It is what mass production does
to a body. Someone sketches a fish on a fountain
and distorts it by stealing a dimension.

Everything stolen wants to buy itself back—
if only as a shell, joined around an armature,
multiplied though remaining one. Until

it is whole again, or more than whole. Giving
and taking like flesh itself, its many versions
around a picnic table, around a pig skewered

and split chin to tail—eyes burnt and dripping
black in the skull. The body turned over flame;
the ecstasy of flesh turned over tongue.

The mouths seem to breathe in the sizzling.
They do. The scent slithers down their throats
before the hand delivers one morsel and the next,

each surrendering less pleasure but still
the need grows. And so a manufacturer
buys a design, takes a mold, and distributes,

at a fraction of the cost of the original,
the same fountain that was before me.
It stood, but the fish, joined at the belly

and split at the pelvis and the gills,
seemed to move, a motion complicated
because the basin was filled with water,

thick and black, like a pupil that absorbs
too much — the pool small, no bigger
than the curls fanning out from a child

as she spins in a yard alone — strange
how it takes only a letter to shift the hunt
to the hunted. To fish. Two fish, no three

curling around a center. The eternal
geometry of binding one and one. God
said, *multiply*, and creation followed. First,

robots weld the skeleton, then concrete
gushes into the mold. Hundreds upon
hundreds a day, drying in a hangar, waiting

for a button to click, for digits to move
one account to another, to make one
with three heads several hundred. Bills

stacked neat, the closed mouths of world
leaders like the locked handle of a safe
where money is no longer held. It takes

some mind to translate art into schematics.
Though the spouts protruded from the fish,
I could not imagine the piping that must

be at the heart. Leaning closer, I saw, spinning
in, a wolf's web — the spider must have traced
its design until the web was thick as the water

that once gushed from the spout. Hiding
in its burrow, on the central nerve-cluster,
the wolf spider once waited — a hand pressed

on a throne's armrest, knuckles curled stiff
and pulsing. Each leg an extended claw.
It felt the insect twitch and knew where

and when to move, to bow ominous music
from the web. The wriggling slowed; the wolf
spider emerged, mouth hidden. It wrapped

and dragged the body inside to inject it
with an enzyme that digests from within.
I can't believe how long I waited. My fingers

numb in the spring cold, tossing bits of bark
into the web. The spider must have died. The web
now a mausoleum in the throats of stone fish.

The caught insects desiccated for nothing,
their exoskeletons now armature in the web.
One death, then many. How deep it must stretch.

Web of web into the center, into the hollow belly
multiplying on its own, by its own design,
wrapping itself with itself, gauze and wound,

body and brain melted into one white blossom
ready to be plucked, ready to wilt and turn
the soil richer, darker like a skull's lost eyes.

ע

We Are Americans

But they — those within
this limousine, a platinum

tooth in the parking lot's
salted smirk — are not. They are

skeletons. At the Mall
of America the open door

twitched like a leg torn
from a cricket. Out they

poured. Some wore ragged
cloth, chains. Others, naked,

did not care. They came to
buy new bodies. We traded.

No, no, no, that won't do, they
say, so we trade again.

The Cormorant

My mother told this story
about a trapped wolf.
Wolf, wolf, over and over,
so I retell it with a cormorant.
Beautiful if a little ungainly,
the bird eats fish, which
wriggle half-out of its mouth,
scales like polished dimes.
The cormorant straightens
its neck, and the living fish
glides down. In the story,
the hungry cormorant stalks
around a fence-line looking
for a way in. It finds none.
It digs. Its hooked beak eats
away the dirt until there is
a hole through which it fits
its head and neck and nothing
more. It slides back and forth
until it rests in an arc of dust.
It rotates its head and sees
a kitchen. From inside, the bird
looks like an odd snake.
Cormorants are semi-aquatic.
Their diving wears away
the soil from the roots.
The trees fall. The cormorant
is pinned. The person grabs
a spade and drives it through
the base of the cormorant's
head — then they see the snake
is feathered like a god or
something cursed, which it is.

The person leaves. The bird
decays. Dirt covers the corpse.
Weeds the dirt. My mother
has been gone a long time.
I like to think she ran away,
if we crossed paths she would
adjust her hair, and I would see
her ears, not as I remember,
but pointed, furred. Her black
eyes, her teeth a single blade,
her beakish nose. I would know
her story. It would hang from
my mouth, a wriggling tale,
when I tell it to my friends.

The Sheet in the Dislocated Room

–*after Richard Siken*

The windows were shattered on many floors so the wind came in and untied
    cables and bits of drywall
before disappearing
        like an ache in the body, growing in time
                                        not larger but more

expected. The building let the wind rub its belly smooth.
    Its doors swung wide: concrete pillars, concrete floors, concrete screws
holding conduits in place,
                and the body said, *No.* The body said,
This is not the plot we sketched for ourselves.
                                But the body
    also thirsted in the semi-abandoned dark.

Here is a canister of spray paint, the rag soaked in chemicals. Here's the PVC pipe
        stretching floor to floor,
                punched through with holes.

Here's a sack of drained Milwaukee's Best, engine in an aluminum tube, the revving
    and the revenant.
Here is the outlet, the room's defunct face; the expressionless dead.

Light stretched across debris—glass, nails, the lost teeth of the building.

        This is the part when I wake up in another person's clothes,
        when I fail to stay inside the building of my own body.

Stay put, said the body, and *I'll bring you something.*
                                            I grew
weary of something so I moved—up stairs, through doors
    up stairs, through wounds

ø ø ø

in the drywall between aluminum studs, until suddenly no floor.
                                        Meanwhile,
something on the lowest story moved like the wind tongued it across the floor and up—

a sheet with folds so fresh they jutted like ribs under the skin
                                        of a crash victim.
Like a shadow of a man throwing his fists
    across a kitchen.
            The sheet came to rest on the stairs—

                                        The wind picked up

and the light dropped down the long hole, story to story.

                    The vertical hallway between here and there
            and the makeshift doors
fabric draped loose from the frames like a drowning body.

The body spoke, and the building replied.
                    The face hung from the brain's hook.

The sheet hovered into the room, edges fluttering. It's night. It's noon.

The wind grew hands
                                that lunged
            and snatched the sheet out of the air like a criminal in the back
            of a convenience store.

Far away, a window shattered, and the light tumbled
        down the building
and onto the highway, where it was taken, car to car, into another city.

ø ø ø

I have been nothing. Nothing
for a long time. Nothing drinking nothing.

And for a moment the body was in paradise
and for a moment the body floated above the sheet.

Then the wind spilled in and pushed the body back.
It lifted the sheet long enough for me
to see its holes as eyes.

I put on the clothes of another person. Midnight. Noon. Morning. Midnight.
I thought I could not speak. I spoke. I could not speak.

Jolene at 33

The speaker's *pleases* bloat.
A drum in the stomach's soft pit.
A guitar strung with rain.
                                        The name

that spins within the sleeping leaps
from another's mouth. The flaming
swells; the fire shrinks, the tongue
                                        unconsumed. Every

comparison reverses this triangle.
The hesitation stretches woman and woman
to man and woman and man.
                                        The deadwax

crackles a coda. The slowing hertz.
On the lip, the word to cue the end.

The Palpitating Wing

I saw my reflection in the subway car's
plexiglass — a dancer in a grey coat. I lifted
lipstick to the dark space and puckered.
Behind me, a man kissed the air. He wetted
his mouth. Then, I was at the conservatory.
At home, I peeled back my shoe's sidewalls,
wagged its silk muscle. A flower bloomed
and wilted within. It held me up. We spun
under the house lights. I palpitated in a mirror.
Winged thing, ciphered animal. In the dressing
room's mirrors, my face. Wrapped in black
elastic, dancers bounced through like a gala's
soft light skipping across sequins, diamonds,
glass. Glasses everywhere. A screaming face
etched in every surface. All I did was look.
The lockstep motion of clapping hands.
Spoon against flute. I saw the improbable
mathematics of a line of dancers practicing
their positions at random. We stretched
our tendons on the bare floor. We arced
our limbs. We posed in cocktail dresses
to applause — its hive-like seizing. Let us
touch a crystal flute, let us bleed Tchaikovsky
until Tchaikovsky drips his iron rosé into us.
On the stairs, under my breastbone, my heart
did a little number. Rapid pump to be adored,
pecked, some torn bread tossed to the water.
On the surface, the ghost hand that threw it
to the swans. The reflection rippled — an arm
like a wing, an eye darting surface to surface
while the body posed as if on stage. It will be.
I will be. I will turn in the spotlight and then
change offstage. In the mirror, the thick lines

cradle my empty face—jaw unhinged, pulled up like a veil crowned with teeth. My chest heaved. My foot in fog. In the orchestral pit, the strings increased their quivering. I counted measures. The beat like heels clopping across the gala's floor to a bronze statue, its face smeared white, its eyes recessed coals plugged into the brow's thick gesture. I adjusted my shift. A woman called me a fucking little whore. Mouth opened. Spinning. In each revolution, I saw the light above the crowd. The bulb's vibrating filament. It sung. It licked every inch. I cascaded across the stage, eyes bloodshot, legs like a swan's coiling neck. The body like a sinking feather. The mind delayed a half-beat. Steps like spit from a sleeping mouth. In the light, I was asleep and wide awake; I slunk to the wings. The dark where the director waited. I rubbed my face on his. We all believed I was a swan and her rival. The stage a bed I belonged in. The completed wound is not open but scarred. We read the skin's raised lettering. I bowed. On the subway's stairs, floodlight. At the top, a shadowed figure. I was its twin. I uncupped my fist; my pulse pumped. It was inside me, still at work, alone in the dark.

As It Was

On my lawn, a black plastic bag
wears the hideous skin

of a large bird—torso fully
defrocked. The meaty folds
                    wince when touched

by breeze. Every house
                    is empty, each
window a dark yawn. In the dark
a body is always slipping

                    unnoticed
                    through a dream.

In my dreams, I fell and jerked

awake. The nerves flashed
                    the mind back.
The body, misinterpreted
to be in danger, feels

in danger. Once I cleaned a catfish
                    on a truck's tailgate.
Its head closest to my body

its flesh spread back from a single slit.

Like a dream right after
some violence,
                    the fish
                    just there.

I sway. Black bag,
                        featherless bird.
The streetlight's clear juices.

The catfish's dying lungs
pulsed though flayed.

Its mouth gasped slower.

The bag like skin
                        like ruined silk.

Beyond my lawn, the opening
door I tuck myself within.

Homunculus

That summer, the whole city smelled of reefer. I leaned back from the table while my neighbor's eyes flowered in the half-light of a lamp placed in the corner. And after that, I sat at my desk and watched the bed sheets stiffen and relax like the face's little muscles. A muscle after a hit. I spoke a big game. About equality. The "sublime." I turned the corner from the restaurant's hallway to where I washed dishes. I saw the owner swing and connect his elbow to his wife's temple. It was my neighbor's birthday. At one time, he beat every chess player in Nebraska. He told us a story about the homunculus in his brain. I said, *My boss beats his wife.* Scratch that. I said *nothing.* I inhaled and inhaled. I turned around and collected the dishes from the bus tub. Who was I to stand up? My feet shrank to less than human proportion. I tripped. The summer bled its slow artery across the horizon. My neighbor poured his drink all over the floor. *My homunculus is easily observable*, he said. He tilted his head so the light flowed into his ear. I peeked in. The owner's wife often held their daughter in a baby wrap. The tiny body stirred. Soon, bulldozers would level the building. I couldn't say where anyone ended up. After work, my friends carried me down the stairs. They tucked me into the night's tender brain.

Automated Teller Ravine

at the bank   I deposit   my hands and withdraw

some water   like a flower that interests
the face cupped   in my hands meets

my face I make me   rain on me my face
remains outside reflected   on the bank 24/7

A Million Tiny Brains

Because when microscopic, one alone will not work
as you and I imagine,
                                        we need a myriad, a number.

That said, many wonder if the tiny brain is meant to be handled
in large groups or if they are, in the wild, solitary. Studies show the brain,

if tiny, will grow restless when gathered. They rub against one another
                                        until overcome by a red mist
or the atomic-lightning-storm of rapture.

                                        Last week, I confessed in a parking lot I haven't always been
the best friend to have. A common line, I know. And common sense

tells us an isolated tiny brain will develop
                                                                its own language, further separating it
from the herd. So when it tries to say—telepathically—

                                                to another that they are alive and that's all
you could hope for, it thinks in ringing echoes and clicks.

No other tiny brain understands when it radiates from its nanocortex,
I love you, tiny brain. No one reaches out to embrace. Rapture and rupture

shake hands in the mind. In the parking lot, in a time of lightning,
                                                you, me, the infinite folds of the large brain in the sky.

Truth is some tiny brains spend their days retelling their tiny-brained
neighbors about a life-defining moment—its everlasting impact.
Yes, I think about my own time of lightning, how common

rapture spreads its mist from a rupturing.
Afterward, I walked home, heavier, less determined. I stayed
up watching bodies

rub their faces clean off. *Poor tiny brain*, my tiny brain mumbles.
I keep it locked in a cylindrical holding tank,
which is filled with some sort of salty solution.

ע

Predator, Too

When enveloped in heat, any anomaly is attributed to heat. The leaves roil as if under a convex lens. Windows shatter. Man after man loses his head. The body, suspended, sees everything as negotiation. Once, I held a bullet between my thumb and index. It was almost weightless. I flicked it up. I caught it and flicked it again. I stared down the metro tracks of a city I'd just arrived in. Its dark mouth spread. It was summer, the hottest on record. Everyone felt like they were melting. The bullet—what a metaphor—both flint and fire. The tip of a joint at the end of an alley is a target in the pupil of an alien machine. *I cannot do that*, I said. I didn't know what I was dealing with. Then it hit me, and out came the sparks.

The Parade of Corpses

Because the crowd had gathered for some time, the babies were crying a sore-throat cry.

No one dared to leave. Not everyday does a town host a parade
of corpses. Some believed it to be magical—all the graves, all the coffin lids
creaking open, the decayed bodies congregating

into a hierarchy no one alive could understand.
Others believed the dead
would be slow—they lacked muscle—and so deserved forgiveness for the delay.

They said, *It's natural for the body to break*. They sat on the sidewalk
with big smiles plastered over their faces.

Others believed magic
granted preternatural vivacity, plots, unquiet minds.
The corpses must be delayed because they were busy

pilfering houses, hanging at the dingy Shell station, smoking pack after pack of Marlboros.

The dead wailed on bone-trumpets and skull marimbas.
Believers couldn't help but frown thinking about all the fun
the dead must be having while they waited,
sweating their asses off, for this bullshit parade.

You want to head out? they asked. *Are you kidding?* they responded, *and let them win.*

The parade brought out a certain type of resentment
in those who did not believe in magic.

They believed the ghouls were building a large float of human bones,
pulled by a rented tractor.

ø ø ø

Some said, Ah, an Olympics of the afterlife. There must be a council that chose our town.

The parade of corpses could help the area economically—with tourism, media,
the leveling of businesses to make a large stadium on the taxpayer dollar,
the expulsion of homeless people, the whole nine yards.

But the students saw the parade as a giant mirror:
their eyes dragged purplish bags, hair unkempt, skin sickly.
They complained about student debt and coursework.
They began drinking early.

Cynics felt inside themselves
a great pain—a limb thrust into frigid water. They knew they must leave.

But why were so many others duped?

There will always be others in a crowd, murmuring about what it will be like,
what death will be like when it comes, if it comes.

The Missing Parents

When they turned up, it was inevitable to ask about sanitation.
Did they fit their heads through a hole in a house's foundation,
or squeeze, as we know they can, through the u-bend of a toilet?
No one could say. We saw them scurry from the overgrown lots
of unfinished developments. Their minivans dotted the gravel
cul-de-sacs. Soon the signs of infestation spread to the suburbs.
In the posh enclaves, housewives saw them first as fat lumps
in the uncut grass, and then as beady eyes in the back of a pantry.
In the beginning, they waited until dark before moving in the open.
They knocked on doors to inquire if their children were there,
if they could see them. *Just for a second*, they pleaded before sullenly
crossing the street to try the next house and the next. It was obvious
they would lower property values so the neighborhood committees
voted unanimously to hire exterminators to remove the missing
parents, to take them to the country and the trailer parks — anywhere
amphetamines had dug trenches — and release them (there they
could nest). Or, as some argued was the most sanitary and humane
reaction, to exterminate them with poisons, or glue traps, or snap
their necks with spring loaded clamps or a professional's glove.
How does it feel, we asked the pros, *to touch the missing parents, to know
where they're going and where they've been?* The children asked us the same.
We answered with textbook certainty, they come from the bad parts
of the city; they are looking for a handout, a shelter, the things
they gave up when they chose to go missing. These children, in turn,
displayed their knowledge to their classmates. *They are poor*, a child said.
They are diseased, another echoed. The epidemic spread its greased pity
along their windpipes. The televisions looped. Somewhere, they were
patrolling the streets, calling the police, the professionals, who sacked
the missing parents and tossed them into their vans. We told them

the missing parents only want to assault our way of life. We explained the dangers of causing trouble for the sake of causing trouble. We tucked them in and disappeared behind their eyelids. In the morning the sun came through the door followed by a social worker to note our cleanliness. *Our progress*, they said. Instead of a mess, we chose to line the foyer with empty sneakers. What a difference that makes.

Tiny Tykes

I smoked drugs in the cemetery. That was the type of year I was having. When the flood rains started, the children tore across the fenced-in yard of the daycare next door, leaving their toys to drown. They pressed their ghost faces against the bay window, each head a mausoleum of itself. *What about the dead?* I asked my mom on the phone. *Do they continue to grind their teeth? Yes*, she responded, *the dead grind their teeth*. In bed, I replayed this conversation until its filmstrip melted into another paranoia. A painful chirp in the other room. In the crib, glowing and warm, my cell phone threw a small tantrum.

The Shaking Matryoshki

When my neighbor died, I had to go in
her house and take stock of what was trash
and what wasn't. It wasn't what I expected—
not the packed hallways of a hoarder. No,
the house was pristine, as if she dedicated
her life to the endless erasure of herself.
Room by room, I curbed what I could until
I reached the master bedroom. The door's
faux-brass knob shone like a monstrous eye.
I opened it. Inside, six tiers of built-in shelves
full of matryoshka dolls. The shelves stretched
floor to ceiling. The dolls, rows deep on each
shelf, kept their insides within. I wanted one
to open and open but as I neared I heard
a shaking. It came from deep in the shelves.
I thought a mouse must have crawled out
of the wall and along the dolls. The golden
hour plowed through the blinds. The dolls
bathed in it. In every color, each painted face
a variation of its neighbor: the blush, rose lips
pinched up, the eyes enlarged and too blue,
two black dots sitting dead center as nostrils.
I didn't breathe, hoping the shaking would stop,
but, no, it grew louder. Some dolls carried
a bouquet or a basket and some, without arms,
wore aprons painted like fields—paisleyed wheat,
the quick brushstroke of a wild flower. I saw one
then another tilt sideways, their arrhythmic
undulations like the mania of a detached tail.
Their painted details first blurred, tessellated,

then threatened to tear apart. Bought from certified dealers or found by rummaging garage sales, the dolls, even in motion, looked marvelous, flawless, as if my neighbor restored them over the years — each chipped surface, each faded pigment. Their insides clicked against their insides, out of time but perfectly so, and the room shook, and the shelves arced and bowed. The dolls rattled until one fell and emptied itself on the bare floor before me.

The Wasted Pupil

—after A Field in England

I've been here before. A walking ghost before purpose
appeared. Eyes rolling, billowing black sleeves, a man
leads a group through a field. His smile shrieks.
The others hold the corded rope tied around his torso.
His arms look severed. They float. He points the way.
I see my reflection in his black robe. The days I babbled
and thought I was called come to mind. In a field,
a forked path rose out of the grasses. The grass dripped
with blood or bile. All night I led myself somewhere
glittering, unknown, unfindable again. I was on
my back. My face churned. I pushed my breath into
heaven. Each night a scream inside a scream. How similar
a dowsing rod and a twig. The man stops, doubles
over. Back then, I was a snout rubbed to a gleam
and thought the light I reflected was mine. They scan
the field. They pass a bottle. Like a party in high school.
Boys getting hammered on pills, a pilfered bottle already
half-drunk, and one always asking, *Where are the girls?*
Crouching, we didn't know. Hard with philosophy,
we tongued the bottle's neck. We watched the grass roil
in the wind—paths gliding like tributaries: one littered
with beer cans, one made with concrete and crushed skulls,
one like hair before lightning strikes. I can't tell which I took
because when I turn around they are so similar. Whose hands
were on the wheel of the car that drove us? Whose hands
wrote this sibyl's etherized devotions? I sobbed a song.
My friend hung out the window and vomited. In memory,
it streams back inside him. On screen, they dig up a skull
and call themselves loyal. The sky's fucked-up pupil,
the brain whirling like wind in a field—I'm different now.
I tell myself I am different as if I could be any different.

Dollar Fugue

My mother tells me to lighten up her voice's tiny

screen in the night like a head wound on a curb
I drink and drink and wait to rise like smoke

into the sky's deep grave I stare meaningfully
at the dark then I stare menacingly

*

at the dark in the mall I felt nocturnal

in a department store I examined a t-shirt
it admitted *There is no finish line* I thought

about capitalism my mother sent a check
I cashed it inside my apartment I flick

*

a switch the lights remain off every

fabric sings to my fingertips the mall's lesser
symphony the mall's fugue it pads across

the carpeted living room diminishes six
months ago my mother slept in a hospital

*

the sun set   for an hour the sun set for another hour

at all hours from her room I could see   over
the exit ramps   on the other side   the mall curled

its spine into its burrow   a menacing purr
like smoke   rose   into the sky's wide nostrils.

The Growing World

I stepped out of a bonfire into a dark alley. My parents pointed at me. Or was it the fire?

My parents taught me flames write their own exhaustion into paper and wood.
The bigger the flame... you get the idea. I should mention my parents

were on fire. Maybe everyone is a little bit on fire.

My parents believed I was a large child. They bought a Boy Scout shirt
that smothered me. I tucked it in. Its tails hung outside my shorts. It hid

in the closet. A flame grows when confined. I vowed to shrink.
Blissed out on B vitamins, I confessed for an entire day

my thoughts. Amazing how thoughts can be a gas-soaked rag shoved in the mouth.

Whose mouth? Not important. My parents held me up. *Can you believe*
how big this child's gotten? They pulled out a smartphone. They snapped

a photo of their little Boy Scout.
My parents wriggled their orange tongues. Every picture is an exhausted chemical.

My face, a bright dot in the endless black, my parents along the curvature of my eyes.

The Impossible Bouquet

The glass vase distorts the stems that twist like the interlocking legs of lovers in a painting. One foot stands on another; a calf bisects a calf. The line that connects one to another unsure and vanishing. But this is a painting of flowers not lovers. You understand. The verdant stems packed like muscles in a retracted wing flexing out. The silver-green lamb's ear droops with baby's breath, the light blue eclipsing the orange mum, whose petals have stretched their furthest and are now brittle and ready to fall from the flower's concealed head—they do not fall, though they are ready. Nearby, the tightened peony like a puckering pink cabbage refuses to bloom. This is misleading. It has bloomed, it will bloom. The peony is empty of all but its intricately folded self. It asks for a hand to peel back its exterior petals, to let it breathe. But paintings do not speak. Neither do flowers. And hands, when it comes to art, do nothing but conceal. A thought is here, but I can't tell what it is. I can see the cockscomb, the flower that is a human brain, hiding in the foliage of the bouquet. In the painter's mind, the blooming from different seasons, the arrangement first sweet then rancid. A calculated balance. What has never touched touches. A carnation like a shriveled scrotum for the white hand of a lily. Each petal elongated into twisted fingers, the faint stem an exhausted wrist. Hands leave to the imagination what is beneath them, so their every gesture is a little obscene. Without hands to play them, the gold trumpets of daffodils herald neither sleep nor death nor their absence. In a painting, life does not progress to death. Though the eye sees it in the vague arc a leaf takes. In the dark, the dark moves. A hand thrusts forward and dissipates. A face scurries from the ceiling to the wall. The eye loses track. Is it not strange, in the painting, the dark background that hulks over the bouquet? The insects that spill from it? Their translucent wings solid only at the joints of their thoraces. The dark contrasts the bright bursts, almost swallowing the bouquet. The orange crocus burns inside forever. It holds the dark, and the dark seeps, where it can, into the leaves. It nests. It has already nested. In the corner, a flower so purple it is almost black. A bat dahlia. Reminder of what lurks, what waits for the ripening to slow and turn to rot. It drinks the rot with its furred muzzle. But this, too, is misleading. In a painting, nothing waits. Just the momentary pause when the eye moves from one petal to another: the wilting heliotrope a white discharge from the green mouth, the daisy dwarfed by the red tulip, whose bloom is marbled like a mollusk. The insects swarm, eager to take the nectar, the juice that comes from the dead, that the gods drink to save themselves from death. The insects steal it away and give it back. One lower to the next like sex. No sex without death or if there is, it is a pounding, acrid affair. The pansies' embers tremble, fade, and rekindle at the edge of the dark as they have done and still do. And above it all, a Japanese chrysanthemum unfolds, its petals' backsides white, but inside a bright red, so this opening looks painful. Each petal like a tooth ripping strips of flesh from another, from itself—this constant flaying, the rush of oxygen across the blood-gorged membrane, the dark heaving in the background, the seasons folding over each other until beginning and end touch like the retracted petals of a morning glory in the hands of the afternoon.

The Awkward Animal

I thought I saw a large branch floating downstream.
It was motionless in the water, but then it moved
its arm-like stubs, stretched its sack of smashed teeth.
For hours, the alligator floated, then unalarmed it slunk
into the reeds. *How charming*, I thought, fully seeing it.
Along a trail, it would be different. Their depthless
reptilian eyes seeing every color under the skin even
at dusk. Once, I lived on a canal. Alligators lined
the bank, invisible until their nostrils broke the surface.
Once, I saw an alligator with a bulging torso, a head
dissolving into the dark. Both ends tapered to nothing.
Too often the eye cannot make sense of what it sees.
The alligator struggled. I left the porch. I expected it
to leap at me like thick lightning. But it twisted listlessly.
Its belly's rapid pulse. A python's smooth coils. Two
creatures fused. A snake's head sprouting legs, a snout
whorling off. A dragon with two types of scales.
The heart is weighed on one, and the brain the other.
The sight and the sense of the sight. Blood in the eye
and blood in the mouth. Where the alligator's head
should have been, the snake's. Its triangle wrenched
wide, feet limp in its mouth's corners. The python
contracted; the alligator pushed against the inside.
I tried to touch it. To hold both at bay and within.
Its tail corkscrewed; it vomited. Then, they were two
again, themselves. The snake cut up on the inside,
the alligator burnt slick by the stomach's juices.

At Dinner

I pull a hair
from my mouth

It's my own hair
At night it leaves
my head

It ties itself up
A knot for ankles

A knot for a waist
The head a knot

My hair sits on a chair
It reclines It scurries
into the dark

to do what I cannot
say but am tied to

A golden eagle
with a snake
in its beak

I find my hair
in the corners

of every room
I am sorry

This is not polite
I just like to imagine
inside my body

a braided muscle
ready to unspool

a wing flicked out
to slow the wind

that is my body
pressed around me
like lips

ע

Eyeing

in some circles people eat fish eyes   a delicacy

or not   the silver circle in the circle
of the silent mouth   I have been in

these circles   showing everyone the coin
on my tongue   I swallowed my eye

Visitation

I saw the satyr in a dream. He huddled in the branches
of a bush, so I could see only a glimpse—a hoof retracted
into shadow, a shining crown followed by a mane, a thigh
covered in thick fur. His fur swayed in one direction but
one that has within it variations like how a crowd in a large
room seen through a hallway might move, each follicle
an individual touched by wind or the music of a tensing
muscle. The satyr foraged, rapidly stripping the branches,
hands like pale creatures turning the black and sweating soil.
I thought if I approached him slowly as one might approach
a stray or a child, he would speak some revelation, but
the scene shifted; I was in a bedroom. The outline of a body
under the covers. The covers first red then black like meat.
No seared smell. Only the longing for a body, a name
to give the shape. I kneeled, bent to look under the bed—
why, I do not know. I don't know why we do anything
in dreams. I saw the spindled legs walking on the other side.
I lifted my head but I was alone. The body gone. I looked
under the bed again. Again the twitching legs, the hooves.
Days later I took a hike through the park to the cemetery,
the bare kind that dot the Midwest; grief is best, I know,
unadorned. With decoration, it becomes habit, a feast
that calls at night. *Get up, come to me.* So our cemeteries are
rectangular, utilitarian. I hiked there. And there he was.
Huddled in the bush before the wrought iron gates—
the furred thighs, a mane, his bare head like a beacon.
He chewed the flowers from bouquets and spat them out.
Flowers from the graves. *How pitiful*, I thought. Flowers
left for the dead are not for the dead at all, and their use

for the living is over. Flowers seem alive but are dead.
Body rooted in the dirt, memory blossoming through.
The satyr chewed the flower's heads clean off. First, I
thought the dead ought to be honored, then I should feel
no disgust. Then I saw it was not a satyr, not a dream.
Or if a dream, it was different—staged, sensible to those
who cannot experience the dreaming. Instead of myth, a man.
The curtain of bushes scratched him, and his skin rose.
His blood mixed with the dirt furring his thighs. He twirled
his goatee with a finger. One eye clouded, the other bright.
In front of the wrought iron gates, his head shook back
and forth in a flattened figure-eight. He gagged like a dog.
I too could feel the bolus move through his windpipe, peek
over his tongue's mound. Then dozens of paper balls came
out and blossomed into deposit slips when they hit the ground.

Altered

A yard is a box with its lid tilted up so anyone can look inside
and get closure. I looked all day

through the gaps in the fence where the wood rotted off
but I could not see my neighbor's yard. She piled stones,

and her pile, I could see now, hollowed out a space. A grotto
behind a grotto. After death, there is always

another box to look into. Inside, a circle of smooth stones.
The stones glistened with slime. Water-dark. It pooled

around them, and the earth slowly swallowed it — a mouth
smeared with food the body wants but has no place for,

or a brain too full to be a vessel for memories
so they gurgle over the lip. I took a breath as I walked the aisle

between folding chairs. I don't remember if the funeral home
smelled like mildew or that's just what I assumed

and that's why I was thinking about yard work while I shook
hand after hand and the music put my insides inside another box.

Towards the end, my mother showed the gaps
in her mouth all day to the window. The stone circle gurgled.

The water bubbled its dark discharge. The gurgling a hymn
swaddled in reverb. I thought the water was dew, and from it

the slime grew down the rocks. But the water oozed
from the rocks, from cracks that had been covered with slime.

It was difficult to stand there, contemplating various nail sizes
during the long blank moments when an old friend recalled

the most routine day as though it were exemplary. I was on
my feet. I was knocked down. Stiff as a board, light as a stone.

The music grew louder; the slime
thickened. The stones throbbed, and their throbbing amplified.

The people filed out; the earth was already full.

Symphonie

Being dead
was appealing

in popular culture,

so my lips twisted
into a syllable

and held it. In the dark,

I came to the spot
where a person
begins. I did

my make-up
like a vampire.

Four long fingers stretched

into the room. Eyes
closed and drifting,

I was 100%
that vamp.

It brought me down

as lovers do —
hands and necks
turned to candy

ø ø ø

in a pulsing mouth.

I raised
one arm and touched

where I felt the most
deaths occur.

When I Was Dangerous

A fang through lips streams dusk over teeth.
A gold coffin in the earth's pocket chews

the misnamed violence of evening like a face.
I stuffed my stuffed mouth with what
lingers: bored idol, mallet, cymbal, fur trench

coat floating in a pool. The body's lowest
points sing in shadow. My tongue erased itself

with earth. A fleshy coffin crowned with teeth
crescendos at the border of shadow and lip.

I wait for my shadow to come back. I wait forever.
All my nerves surrender with a zap. To my fur —
goodbye shadow cascading into an outline

of its creator. Gold needle, electric tongue.
Gold fang, burnish me into blood.

The Curtain that Extended into the Sky

–*after* Mulholland Drive

Pacing the dim stage, a man said, *It's all recorded.*
Two people walked to their seats. Where I was,
It's all recorded came from the speaker. On screen
two people flinched in the aisle from the voice.
He gestured at the red curtain. I watched as they
watched. That's not it. They watched the bare stage
fill with fog, muted trumpets, an exhausted song.
I watched the stage undo itself and carried within
me the undoing as a tape carries within it a fiction
it makes into fact. The fog cleared. On stage,
a microphone. The man echoed, *It's all recorded.*
The two characters were in disguise. The same
disguise actually. They changed their names. One
or both were dead. Silence seeks a space inside
the flesh when one sense burns for an audience
for its burning. Above the curtain, a plaster arch,
and above that another arch ate into the ceiling,
so the curtain seemed to extend beyond the scalloped
roof into the sky. It was an arts theatre. Static
crawled down the walls, and the projector was on
its last leg. I forgot how long I sat in the theatre.
I turned to the others. I heard their gasps—a certain
removal triangulating uncertainty. Earlier, an actor
sang in a recording booth that wasn't a recording
booth but a set for a film and her singing a recording
of someone unseen. I was dazzled by the timing—
like an uninterrupted track the actors memorized
so their movements and the sound would sync.

I know in the back of a theatre technicians bridge
the stage and auditorium with the soundtrack.
But this is a movie. So no technician. The actors
pretend; the sounds dubbed in. In Hollywood,
everything is mediated. I'm not in Hollywood.
I was once, and there was no glitz except what
I superimposed over campers parked along turnpikes.
I stared until the world rippled with blue and white
lights on top of the curtain on screen. I thought,
Is this not an act? I gripped my chair. Heavy fade,
the microphone whisked away. The low rumble
of breath within, a brief pause between. It is so
hard to tell what is and isn't an act, what voice
within a tape, a machine, and an audience within
a voice without a part to play and whose silences
orchestrate inside the flesh a fiction. Then two
hands thrust through the curtain, facing opposite,
ready to split the curtain and reveal a chest heaving
under a sequined shirt. This didn't happen. Or
it did, but only in my imagination. The curtain
parted, so too the hands drifted. The hands
of two people who practiced matching speed.
Between them, a stool, a radio, its antennae
extended. A third hand appeared. It turned
the radio's large knob: music distorted beyond
recognition until all was the warbling of AM
prophets. I'm so far from the film—my mind
a nesting doll inside another inside another.
The hand fiddled with the knob until the sounds
crystallized. Then the radio clicked off and rumbled.

The Tape-Recorder

When my brain was a mass of static, I wanted a disembodied hand
to creep through the door and cast its filmy glow across the walls

of the attic I slept in, to follow the right angles of exposed rafters
like breaking over and over until the phone would ring and a voice

would emanate from the white noise on the other end. I waited
under a floor lamp as the screen's cold light showed for a moment

a heavily made-up face then the dark, and in the dark the holes
of my eyes. The two faces became one, and then I believed it was

inevitable that a ghost would waltz in as if on a rolling platform—
a static body cruising across the stage before my frameless mattress.

I was crucified on pillows, feet twisted in sheets. The morning
was not yet an idea in the horizon's thick skull when the ghost

arrived. It was a sheet-with-eye-holes affair, solidly disappointing.
Defined edges and no ethereal glimmer, the ghost was a prop

carted in and left. It blocked the television behind it. *Who are you?*
I asked the ghost. *Who are you*, the ghost echoed, becoming even

more inadequate. I supposed it's relevant to state I was between
jobs at the time and with little aspiration. Someone told me that

I was the type of person who looks at a mirror and not into it.
It was a season of reflection for me. Then the ghost whirred

0 0 0

and parted the sheet. Inside, a tape-recorder. Its reels turned
like eyes when the machinery of the brain focuses on messages

scrambled in magnetic pulses. The tape seeped out of the recorder.
When it spoke again, I heard my voice harmonized with car horns

and the amplified sound of decaying plants. The ghost stood still.
It was so corporeal I believed my mouth was somewhere within.

Without a Leash

The dog raised his head
over the fence. Night filled
with the dog's star-like teeth.
What came to mind was
creature, the cage the word
makes of teeth underneath
lips, tongue pacing the roof
of the mouth. A swallowed
hiss. *Creature*. The dog was
brindled as night is brindled
when one looks through it—
its emptied pockets striped
with weak light, the road
like a ribbon sinking into
a dark pool. I thought
about my habit of walking
the distance between one
streetlight and another,
the hands that lurk there,
the angry work they do.
True, I have difficulties
sleeping and so prowl,
though not like this dog
barking at any moving thing;
his barking called the other
dogs, unseen in unlit yards,
to join without knowing
object of their cries.
I was the object. I made
them howl. They didn't see
me. Instead, they made me
a note in their lurching
chorus. The dog's head

dangled over the fence.
The planks pushed into
his neck, his fur. His head
hung there, impaled,
without a body, shrieking
though not in pain as one
might expect, but in deep
anger. How did it get there?
The dog's head. The fence.
His master, no doubt—
the man who built the fence
seven feet high, who placed
the dog inside and stood
at the gate, rattling a can
of pennies near his dog's
ear, maybe smacking him
a couple times to say,
Those out here aren't good
Scare them or suffer. Or
so I thought. The dog
preferred not to suffer,
preferred his own voice
to a planted threat. *Creature*—
to be made but for what?
To feel wrapped in another's
handiwork. The dog focused
on me. My purpose was clear
to him. His to me. The dog
fell back behind the fence.
I was in a part of the city
where houses dotted one
side of the highway, and
body shops the other—

both with dogs behind
their fences. The highway
like a fence for the city.
I paced its edge. I could
hear the snarling. The dog
raised his head over the fence,
his hackles in the streetlight
that was not quite red, and not
orange but an odd mix that
animates the inanimate dark.
His coat made it odder still
as it spilled over the dog,
looking down, as if standing
on his hind legs; I know this
is not possible. The fence
stood seven feet. The dog
rested his paws there—
larger than a dog, or a man.
It was as if he were both
at once. Night creature,
strange hybrid—but not
the moon's changeling,
not the alternation between
two. The two inhabiting
the same body, the lonely
whose fur sprouts from human
skin, whose human feet contort
into the backward-jointed
legs of a dog. The two-toned
torso: back covered in fur
and the front with twisted abs
like a saint carved from stone,
eyes to God's unfathomable

wrath unfurling above the earth.
A moment only, and then
the dog returned to itself.
A brindled dog, alerting
his master as his master
undoubtedly trained him
to do. To be another's never
knowing, and now, the dog
barked whenever he could.
God, I thought, *looking down*
at the dog looking down at the street.
The anger exhaled from
one mouth into the other.
The master plotting a beer
bottle's trajectory so it would
strike the dog like a holy bolt
of lightning and silence him.
So unnerved was the master.
I squeezed my fists. I let
them slacken. I felt a stranger's
hands chain me to my body.
Behind the wooden fence,
the dog perpetually shifted.

Acknowledgments

The Account: “The Palpitating Wing” [nominated for Best New Poets Anthology], “The Suspended Body” [semi-finalist for the Palette Poetry Previously Published Poem Contest]

Arc Poetry: “We Are Americans”

Arkansas International: “Homunculus”

Bennington Review: “The Missing Parents”

Broadsided: “The Complicated Thing” [nominated for Best of the Net and Pushcart Prize]

The Chicago Review: “Predator Too,” “Automated Teller Ravine”

Coal Hill Review: “The Sheet in The Dislocated Room”

CutBank: “The Parade of Corpses”

december: “Visitation”

decomP: “Who Cannot Place Themselves in The Soul of The Hunter”

DIAGRAM: “Consumption,” “The Shaking Matryoshki”

Fantastic Floridas: “In Florida,” “Awkward Animal”

Foundry: “Who Are Americans”

Golden Walkman: “Scarlet Heaven” (included in The New Anthology of Contemporary Surrealist and Magical Realist Poetry)

Honey Literary: “The Master in Pieces”

The Hunger: “The Cormorant”

Jet Fuel Review: “To Bury Everything,” “The Dybbuk” [nominated for Best of the Net]

Landlocked: ‘Symphonie”

The Laurel Review: “Receive with Simplicity Everything that Happens,” “Without a Leash”

Mercurius: “At Dinner,” “Tiny Tykes,” “Cyclist with Parachute,” “Metastatic,” “The Dark Radio”

Osmanthus: “Imagining a Thing that does Not Look like a Ghost”

Pacifica Lit Mag: “*Jolene* at 33”

Palette Poetry: “A feast of small proportions”

Pangyrus: “Altered”

Poetry Northwest: “The Curtain that Extended into The Sky”

Portland Review: “The Wasted Pupil”

Quarterly West: "The Impossible Bouquet"
Southern Indiana Review: "Eyeing"
Stirring: "When I was Dangerous," "A Million Tiny Brains"
Timber: "The Dad"
Waxwing: "As it Was"
Writer's Foundry Review: "The Growing World"

Some of these poems are included in the chapbook *A Feast of Small Proportions* (Fork Apple Press, 2026)

Rivka Clifton is the transfemme author of *Muzzle* (JackLeg Press, 2025) as well as the chapbooks *MOT* and *Agape* (Osmanthus Press). Clifton's work has appeared in *Pleiades*, *Guernica*, *Black Warrior Review*, *Colorado Review*, and other magazines. She lives in Seattle.

Colophon

The headers of *Wrong Feast* are set in **Sunbather**, "a 'beyond high contrast' typeface originally designed by Nick Steinhardt for the now iconic 2013 Deafheaven album cover of the same name.

"Referencing early 20th century experiments by Swiss typographer Jan Tschichold, Sunbather challenges your eye to infer what isn't there. Sinewy curves meet sharp serifs to entrance the viewer's gaze.

"The regular weight stays true to the original font, while an added lowercase, diacritics, and stylistic alternates allow you to change terminal shapes or add in serifs that were purposefully omitted in the original."

—deathwishinc.com, 2026

The body of *Wrong Feast* is set in Baskerville URW.